# 51 things to make with Toilet Rolls

## Fiona Hayes

QED

# Contents

## Basic Equipment

Most of these projects use some or all of the following equipment, so keep these handy:

- **PVA glue**
- **Scissors**
- **Pencils**
- **Ruler**
- **Felt-tip pens**
- **Paint brushes**
- **Clothes pegs**

Unless specified, short cardboard rolls are used.

# Giraffe

This cute giraffe will turn your bedroom into a safari wonderland! You could even make a herd of them!

**1** Cut the corner off two short toilet rolls and one long roll.

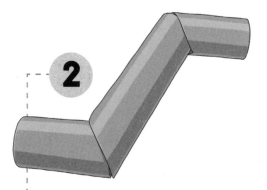

**2** Glue the rolls together, as shown. They should slide into each other a bit.

**3** Cut the corner off another two toilet rolls to make the legs. Glue the legs to the body.

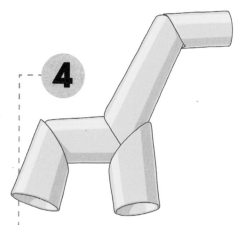

**4** Paint the rolls yellow, then when completely dry, add some brown spots.

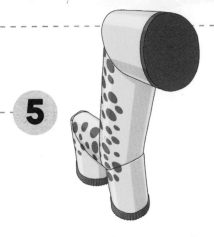

**5**

Glue a circle of brown card to the front of the head. Glue some thin strips of brown card to the bottom of the legs, for hooves.

**6**

Glue a narrow strip of card along the back of the neck, for the mane. Cut ears from leftover card and two short sections off the straw for the horns. Glue in place.

**7**

Add a smile. To make the eyes stand out, add coloured felt circles before you stick on the eyes. Your giraffe is ready!

### Handy Hint

Slightly flatten the toilet rolls to make them easier to cut.

# Lovely Lion

ROAAAR! Who's the king of the jungle? This gorgeous yellow lion! Put it at the foot of your bed to guard all your toys.

## You will need

**Five toilet rolls**
**Thick card**
**Yellow paint**
**Brown card**
**Two googly eyes**
**One black pompom**

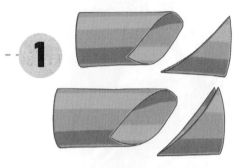

**1** Cut the corner off one end of two toilet rolls.

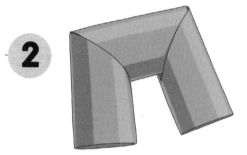

**2** To make the body, glue the rolls to either end of another roll, as shown. They should slide into each other a bit.

**3** Cut a ring from another roll. Glue it to the body, to make the neck.

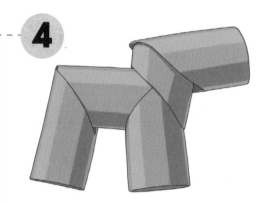

**4** Cut the corner off the last roll and glue it to the neck. This is the head. Add a circle of thick card to the end of the head. Paint the lion yellow.

**5**

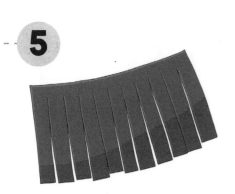

Cut slits along a strip of brown card. This will be the mane.

**6**

Glue the card in place. You may need two strips to make a really thick mane.

**7**

Add some googly eyes, a pompom nose and a smile! Can you hear the lion roar?

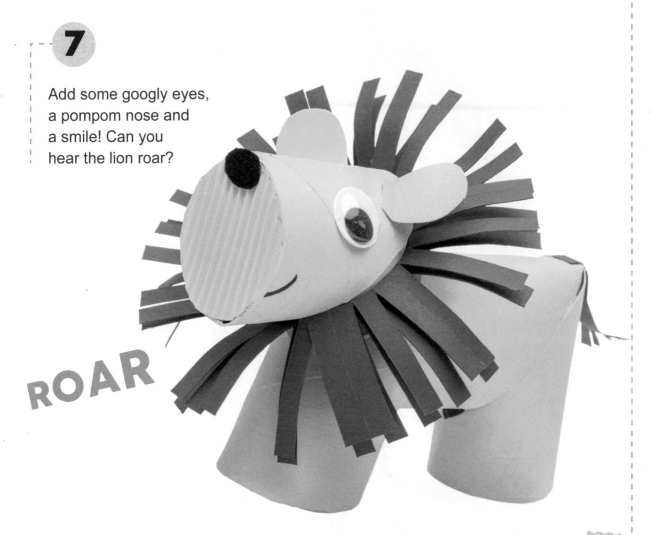

ROAR

# Bird House

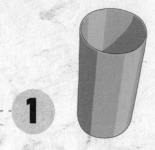

**1** Paint a toilet roll any colour you choose.

**2** To make the roof, cut a semi-circle from card. Glue a piece of string in the middle, as shown.

**3** Roll the semi-circle into a cone and glue the edges together. Make sure the string extends from the pointed end. Hold in place with a peg and leave to dry.

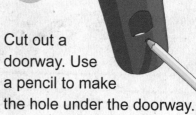

**4** Cut out a doorway. Use a pencil to make the hole under the doorway.

**5** Glue the roof to the base.

**6** For the perch, glue on a short length of straw. Why not make a few houses and hang them up together?

# Bouncy Bunny

**1**

Cut two narrow rings from a toilet roll. These will be the ears.

**2**

Paint another toilet roll and the ears brown.

**3**

Press the ears together and glue in shape.

**4**

Glue the ears onto the top of the other roll.

**5**

Cut out a circle of felt, for the tummy. Glue in place.

**6**

Add a nose, googly eyes and a happy smile. Use different coloured paint to make some friends for your rabbit.

9

# Chickens

Cluck, cluck, cluck! These pretty, spotty chickens will brighten up any room. You could make a set and line them up on a shelf.

## You will need

**Two toilet rolls**
**Paint**
**Red felt or card**
**Yellow card**
**Four googly eyes**

**1**

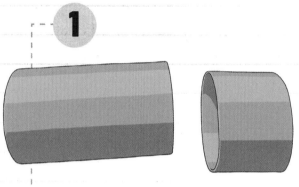

For each chicken, cut a toilet roll, as shown. Use the longer pieces for your chickens and recycle the rest.

**2**

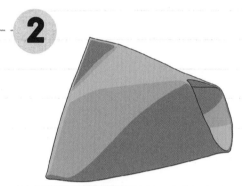

Flatten one end of each roll and glue it together.

**3**

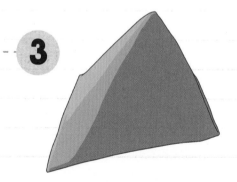

Flatten the other end of each roll the opposite way to step 2, and glue it together. Paint your chickens.

**4**

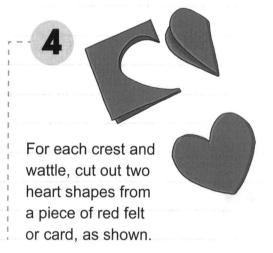

For each crest and wattle, cut out two heart shapes from a piece of red felt or card, as shown.

**5**

Fold in half
a piece of
yellow card
and cut out
a triangle,
for the beak.

**6**

Glue the
crest, wattle
and beak
in place.

**7**

Paint your chicken. Add
spots and googly eyes and
cluck, cluck, cluck!

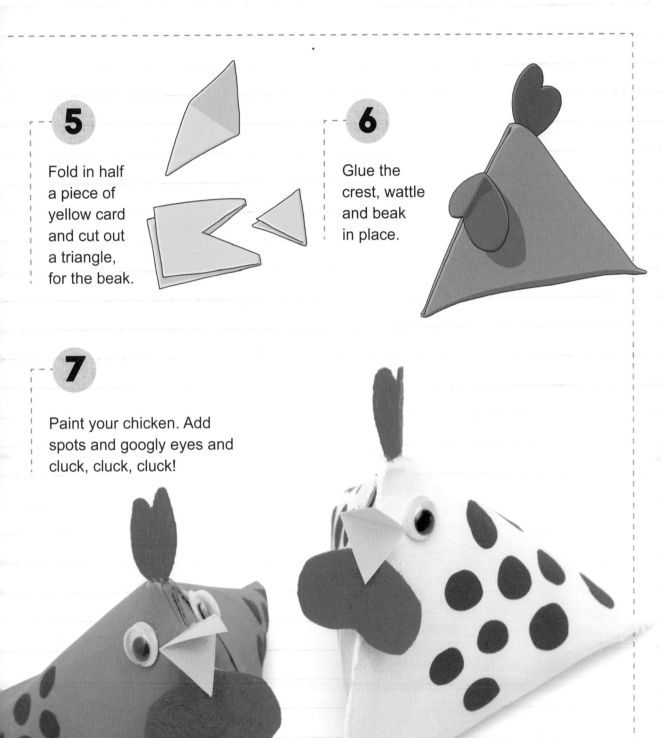

CLUCK

CLUCK

# Daisies

Do you love flowers? If you do, you will adore these beautiful daisies. Make a bunch of them and put them in a vase.

## You will need

Two toilet rolls
Paint, including green
Elastic band
Thick card
Tissue paper

**1**

To make one flower, paint two toilet rolls on the inside and outside.

**2**

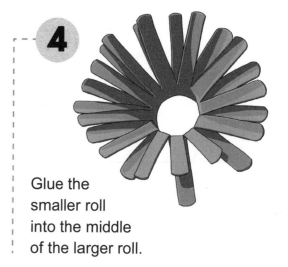

Put an elastic band around the top of each roll, as shown. Cut slits up to the band.

**3**

Bend the pieces outwards, to make petals. Cut one of the rolls, to make the diameter slightly smaller, and re-glue.

**4**

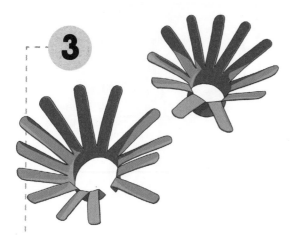

Glue the smaller roll into the middle of the larger roll.

**5**

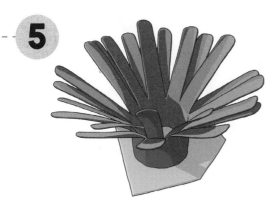

Glue the back of the daisy to a piece of card. When dry, cut away the excess card and paint it green.

**6**

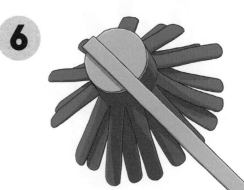

Glue a narrow strip of thick card to the back of the daisy for the stem. Paint it green.

**7**

Scrunch up some tissue paper and glue it into the middle of the flower to finish off the pretty bloom.

# Dragonfly

What is pretty, brightly coloured and flits around a garden pond? A beautiful dragonfly! Make a cute little friend, or two or three!

## You will need

**One short toilet roll**
**One long cardboard roll**
**Paint**
**Bubble wrap**
**Felt**
**Two googly eyes**

**1**

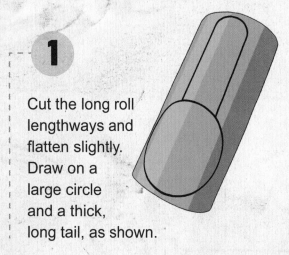

Cut the long roll lengthways and flatten slightly. Draw on a large circle and a thick, long tail, as shown.

**2**

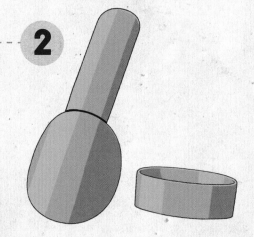

Cut out the shape. Cut a narrow ring from the short roll.

**3**

Paint on your design – stripes or spots will look good. Don't forget to paint the narrow ring too. Leave to dry.

**4**

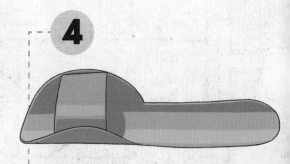

Glue the narrow ring underneath your dragonfly's body. Use clothes pegs to hold it in place until dry.

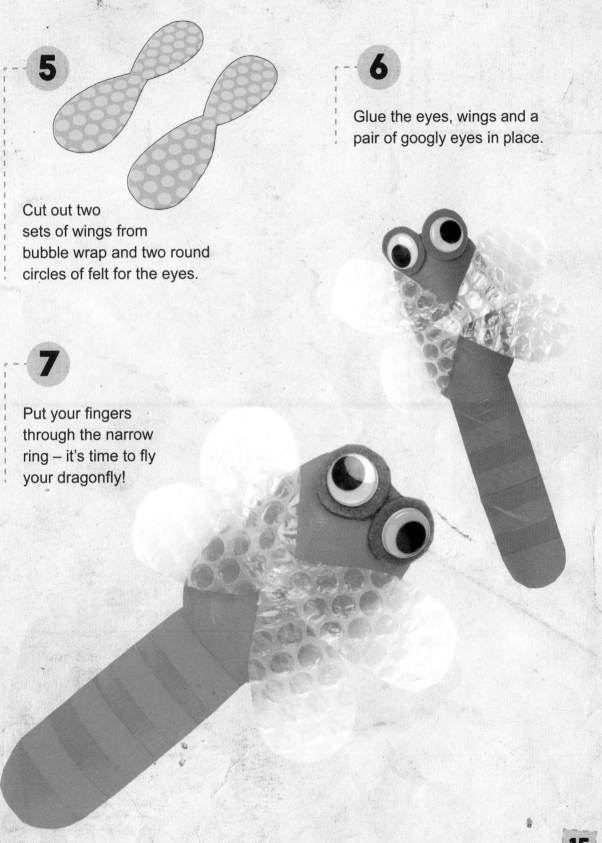

**5**

Cut out two sets of wings from bubble wrap and two round circles of felt for the eyes.

**6**

Glue the eyes, wings and a pair of googly eyes in place.

**7**

Put your fingers through the narrow ring – it's time to fly your dragonfly!

# Cute Duck

Quack, quack, quack!
This gorgeous little duck
is lots of fun to make and
even more fun to play with!

## You will need

**Three toilet rolls**

**Yellow and orange paint**

**Thick card**

**Googly eyes**

**1**

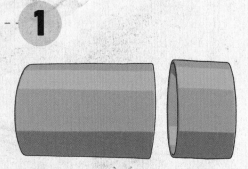

Cut a toilet roll, as shown. Keep
the larger section for the duck's
legs, recycle the smaller bit.

**2**

To make the head, cut out a
long, curved V from one end
of another roll.

**3**

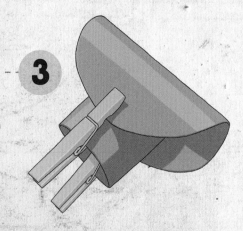

Cut a large oval from another
toilet roll. Glue the legs to the
underside. Hold in place with
clothes pegs until dry.

**4**

Glue the head to the
top of the body.

## 5

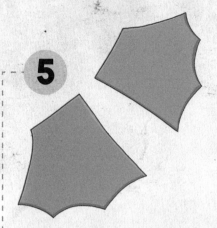

Cut out a pair of webbed feet from the thick card and paint them orange.

## 6

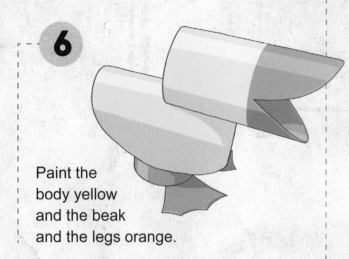

Paint the body yellow and the beak and the legs orange.

QUACK
QUACK

## 7

Add some googly eyes to finish off this cute and colourful duck!

# Cake and Candles

## You will need

At least 12 toilet rolls

Paint, including white and brown

Yellow and white card

Thick card

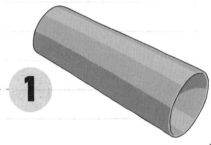

### 1
For each candle, cut a small strip of thick card the same width as a toilet roll. Glue this strip into one end of the roll.

### 2

Paint the candle. Cut out a flame shape from yellow card. Glue it to the strip in the middle of the candle.

### 3
To make the cake, cut out two large circles from thick card.

### 4

Cut about six toilet rolls in half, to make 12 halves.

### 5
Glue the toilet roll halves around the inside edge of one of the circles.

### 6
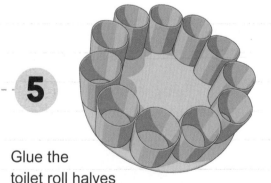
Glue the other circle on top, as shown.

**7**

Cut a strip of white card. Keep one edge straight but make the other wobbly. This will be the cake icing.

**8**

Glue the icing around the top edge of the cake. Paint the top white and the rest of the cake a chocolate-brown.

**9**

Glue the candles in place. Your birthday cake is ready ... Happy birthday to you!

**Handy Hint**
Use a piece of card as a spatula to spread glue.

# Super Specs

If you love glasses and fun accessories, you will love these wild and wacky specs!

**You will need**

Two toilet rolls
Paint
Thick card

**1**

Cut a toilet roll in half. Paint both pieces – use a different colour on the insides.

**2**

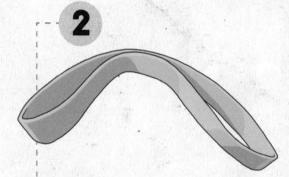

Cut a narrow section from another toilet roll and paint it the same colour as the outside of the rolls. Bend it a little.

**3**

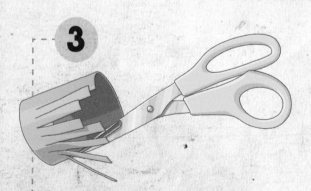

Cut slits along one edge of each toilet roll half, as shown.

**4**

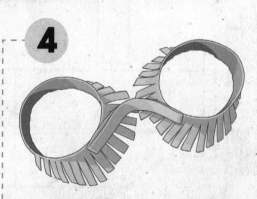

Glue the narrow section to the solid parts of the rolls.

**5**

Cut out two arms from thick card, and paint.

**6**

Glue the arms to the outside edges of the rolls. Put on your glasses – how do you look?

TOO COOL

# Pretty Fish

What's brightly coloured, swims
under the sea and blows bubbles?
This cute fish!

**1**

Cut out a curved V from
the end of a toilet roll.

**2**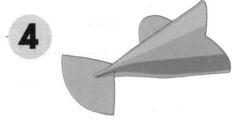

Flatten the opposite
end and glue the
edges together.

**3**

Cut a fin and tail from thick
card. Cut a slit in the tail, so it
will slide onto the end of the fish.

**4**

Use a pencil to make a hole for
your scissors on the top. Cut a
slit on the top, for the fin to slide
into. Glue the tail and fin in place.

**5**

Paint the fish with
spots or stripes. Add
some googly eyes.
Why not make a
whole shoal of fish
and hang them up?

# Flowers

Did you love making the daisies on page 12? Here are some more beautiful blooms to add to them.

**1**

To make each flower, lightly compress a roll and draw on five evenly spaced lines. Cut along the lines to make six rings.

**2**

Squeeze the rings so they look like petals.

**3**

Glue the rings together to make a flower, as shown. Hold in place with clothes pegs until dry. Paint your flower.

**4**

Make a stem for your flower by rolling a thin piece of green paper around a pencil. Start from the corner and roll diagonally until the end. Slide out the pencil before you glue the paper in place. Glue the stem to the middle of the flower.

**5**

Repeat steps 1 to 4 to make more flowers. Glue a circle of card to the centre of each flower. You can bend the stems to angle your flowers.

# Toothy Shark

Is it safe to go swimming today? Well, this smiling, speeding shark won't harm you! You could put it in your bathroom to scare your guests, though!

## You will need

**One long cardboard roll**

**Grey and white paint**

**Blue and white felt**

**Two googly eyes**

**1**

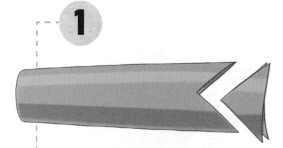

Slightly flatten a long roll so it is easier to cut. Cut out a V from one end. Keep this piece for the tail and fin.

**2**

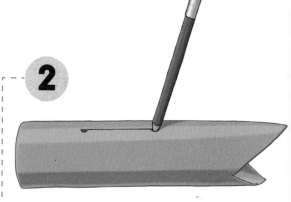

Using a pencil, make a hole in the long piece of roll. Then cut a slot for the fin to slide into.

**3**

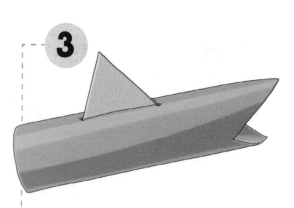

Glue the fin in place.

**4**

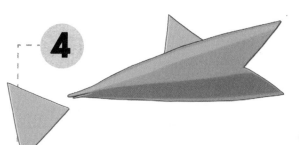

Flatten the uncut end of the roll, glue the edges together. Cut a slit in the tail and slide onto the back of the shark.

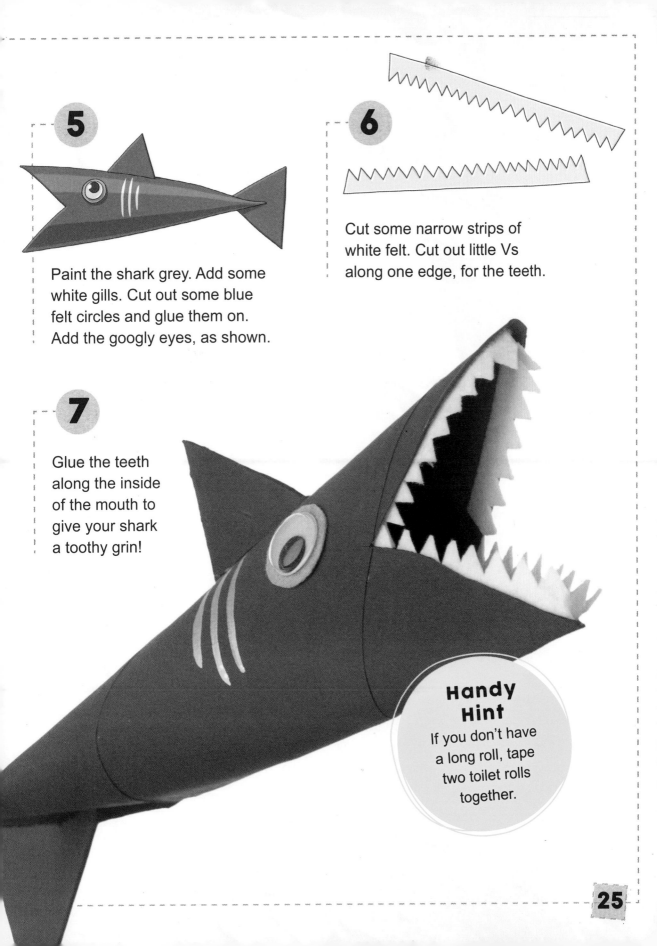

**5**

Paint the shark grey. Add some white gills. Cut out some blue felt circles and glue them on. Add the googly eyes, as shown.

**6**

Cut some narrow strips of white felt. Cut out little Vs along one edge, for the teeth.

**7**

Glue the teeth along the inside of the mouth to give your shark a toothy grin!

### Handy Hint
If you don't have a long roll, tape two toilet rolls together.

# Train

Make this multi-coloured train – it will be the best on any track.

## You will need

Five toilet rolls

Thick card

Tube top

Paint

Ribbon

**1**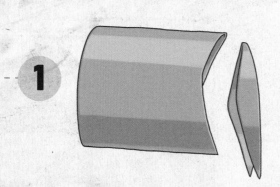

Cut out a curved section from one end of a toilet roll.

**2**

Glue the curved edge to the side of another roll.

**3**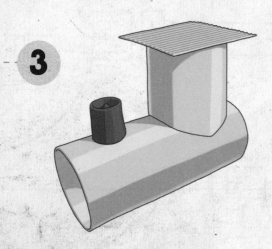

Glue a square of thick card to the top. Paint the train engine a lovely bright colour. Add a tube top for the funnel, as shown.

## Handy Hint

To make a circle, draw around a jar lid and cut out.

**4**

Paint three other rolls for the carriages. To make wheels, cut out four circles of thick card for each carriage and six circles for the engine. Paint and glue them into position.

**5**

Cut some pieces of ribbon. Glue to the inside of the engine and carriages, as shown.

**6**

Make a long line of carriages for the train to pull!

CHOO
**CHOO**

# Friendly Fox

**1**

Fold the top of a toilet roll, as shown. Glue in place.

**2**

Paint the top part of the roll brown and the underneath white. Paint on a black nose.

**3**

Cut out two triangles from the card, for ears. Paint them brown and glue them in place.

**4**

Add two googly eyes, whiskers and other details. Quick, hide the chickens!

# Frog

## You will need

**One toilet roll**
**Green and yellow paint**
**Two googly eyes**

**1**

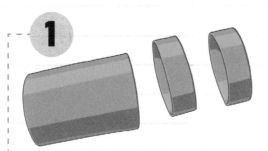

Cut two narrow rings from a toilet roll.

**2**

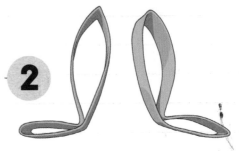

Flatten the rings and fold, as shown, to make the legs.

**3**

Glue the legs to the body.

**4**

Paint your frog green, with a yellow tummy.

**5**

Add some eyes and a smile... Ribbet, ribbet, your frog is ready!

29

# Chinese Lanterns

## You will need

**One toilet roll**
**Paint**
**Card**

**1**

Paint the inside and outside of a toilet roll and cut it along its length.

**2**

Flatten the roll and fold in half lengthways. Cut slits from the folded edge, as shown. Don't cut to the top!

**3**

Re-roll the roll and glue the edges together.

**4**

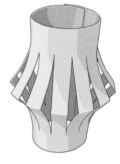

Lightly compress the roll, to make the slits fold out.

**5**

Cut a thin strip of card for a handle and glue to the top of the lantern. Use clothes pegs to hold in place.

**6**

Your lantern is ready. Make lots more lanterns and hang them up with string.

# Totem Pole

**1**

Paint three toilet
rolls different colours.

**2**

Cut and paint two strips of thick
card. Glue the card around the
rolls, making one long, sturdy roll.

**3**

Cut out a rectangle from
thick card. Cut a curved
edge into one side of
the rectangle, as shown.
Paint. Cut two slits in the
top of the first roll. Push
the rectangle into the slits.

**4**

Cut a circle from the thick card and
paint it. Glue it over the top roll. Add
felt circles, googly eyes, beaks and
scary mouths made from thick card.

# Caterpillar

This cute and colourful caterpillar will brighten up any bedroom. Why not hang it from your ceiling?

## You will need

**Five toilet rolls**
**Paint, including red**
**Ribbon**
**One polystyrene ball**
**Two googly eyes**
**Two bendy straws**

**1** Paint some toilet rolls different colours. When dry, cut the rolls into three sections.

**2** Place the cut rolls side by side – mix up the colours. Glue a long piece of ribbon to the top of each roll.

**3** Paint a roll red, and when dry, cut it into thin rings, as shown.

**4**

Glue the narrow red rings onto the ribbon. Turn over so the ribbon is on the bottom.

## 5

Paint a polystyrene ball and glue it to the front of your caterpillar. Add some googly eyes.

## 6

Use a pencil to make two holes on the top of the ball. Insert two short straws and glue in place. Your creepy, crawly caterpillar is ready!

### Handy Hint

Allow the glue to dry completely before moving your caterpillar.

# Awesome Owls

**1**

To make each owl, push in the sides of the top of a toilet roll, as shown, and paint it a bright colour.

**2**

From felt, cut out two wings and an orange beak.

**3**

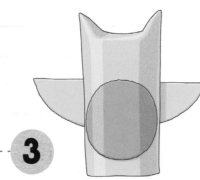

Cut a circle out of felt and glue it in place, as shown. Glue the wings in place.

**4**

Glue the beak in place. Cut out two circles of felt – they should be slightly larger than the eyes. Glue the eyes to the felt, then glue onto the owl. Cut a small slit into either side of your owl, so you can stand it on a tree branch. Repeat steps 1 to 4 to make two more owls.

**5**

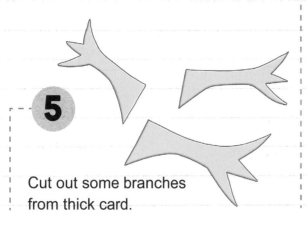

Cut out some branches from thick card.

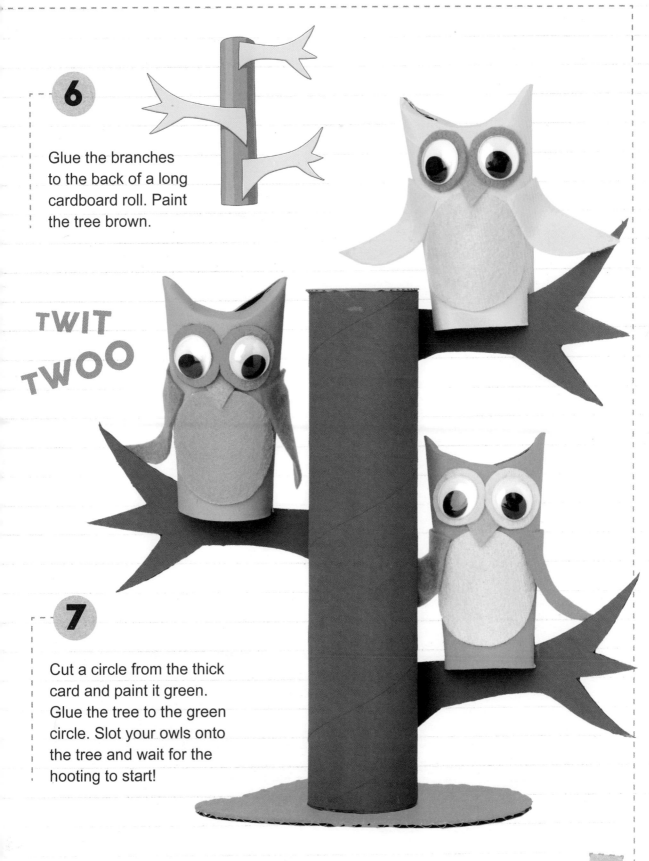

**6**

Glue the branches to the back of a long cardboard roll. Paint the tree brown.

TWIT TWOO

**7**

Cut a circle from the thick card and paint it green. Glue the tree to the green circle. Slot your owls onto the tree and wait for the hooting to start!

# Pencils

**1**

Paint a toilet roll. Glue the bottom to a piece of card.

**2**

When dry, cut away the excess card.

**3**

Cut out a semi-circle from a piece of card. Use wobbly scissors, if you have some, to cut along the curved edge.

**4**

Roll the card into a cone and glue together. Hold in place with a clothes peg until dry.

**5**

Paint the top of the cone the same colour as the base. Repeat these steps to make a whole set of pencils. To make them different sizes, just cut pieces off the rolls before you start.

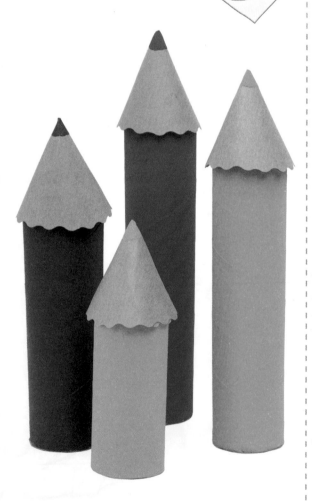

# Sausage Dog

## You will need

**One short toilet roll**
**One long cardboard roll**
**Paint, including black**
**Thick card**
**Two googly eyes**

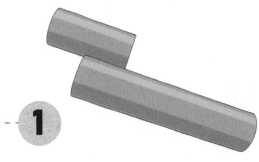

**1** Glue a short roll to a long one, as shown.

**2** From thick card, cut out four legs, as shown.

**3** Glue the legs in place. Paint the dog.

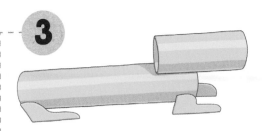

**4** Cut out two ears and a tail from thick card. Paint them a contrasting colour.

**5** Glue the ears and tail in place. Cut out a small circle and paint it black, for the nose. Cut a small slit in the top of the head and slide the nose in place. Glue to hold in position. Add some googly eyes and a smile. Your little pooch is ready to play!

# Octopus

This amazing octopus looks so great that you'll feel you are exploring the deep for real!

## You will need

One toilet roll
Paint
Elastic band
Two googly eyes

**1**

Paint a toilet roll inside and out. Use a contrasting colour on the inside.

**2**

Put an elastic band around the roll, as shown. Cut eight evenly spaced slits up to the band.

**3**

Remove the band and roll each section around a pencil.

**4**

Now your octopus has eight legs.

**5**

Paint on some spots and a smile, and add some googly eyes to this eight-legged sea creature.

# Tractor

## You will need

Two toilet rolls
Paint
Thick card
Blue card
One tube top

**1**

Cut out a curved
section from one end of a toilet roll.

**2**

Glue the curved
edge to the side
of another roll.

**3**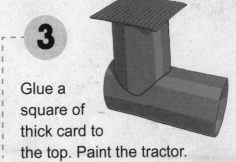

Glue a
square of
thick card to
the top. Paint the tractor.

**4**

For wheels, cut
out two large and two
small circles from thick
card, and paint them.

**5**

Glue the wheels
to the sides of
the tractor.

**6**

Add some card rectangles for
windows. Glue a tube top to
the front for the chimney.

# Mini Mice

Are you scared of mice? Well, there is nothing scary about these cuddly friends. You'll want to make lots and lots of them!

## You will need

**Two toilet rolls**

**Light grey, dark grey and pink paint**

**Pink felt**

**Four googly eyes**

**1** Flatten one end of a toilet roll and glue the sides together.

**2** Flatten the other end the opposite way to step 1, and glue the sides together. Repeat steps 1 and 2 with another toilet roll.

**3** Paint the mice, as shown – don't forget the noses! Cut out some ears and a tail from pink felt, glue in place.

**4** Glue on some googly eyes and wait for the happy squeaks to begin!

40

# Pink Piglet

Snort, grunt, snort, grunt! It's piglet-making time – have fun!

**1**

Push the sides of a toilet roll into the centre, to create a curved top. Paint the roll pink.

**2**

Wrap a thin strip of pink card around a pencil to curl it into a tail.

**3**

Cut out an oval of pink felt for the snout, paint on some nostrils and glue it in place. Glue on the tail and some googly eyes with blue felt circles.

OINK OINK

# Red Squirrel

You have probably seen lots of grey squirrels, but red squirrels are far rarer – and very, very beautiful, just like this one!

## You will need

**Two toilet rolls**

**Orange, dark brown, black and white paint**

**Two googly eyes**

**Thick card**

**1**

Push the sides of a toilet roll into the centre, to create a curved top. Paint light brown.

**2**

Cut three narrow rings from another toilet roll. Paint light brown.

**3**

Bend two rings as shown, for the legs. Cut the last ring in half, for the arms.

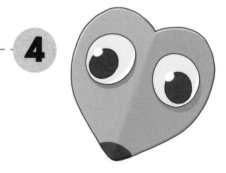

**4**

Cut out a heart shape from thick card and lightly fold down the middle. Glue on some googly eyes and paint on a small nose.

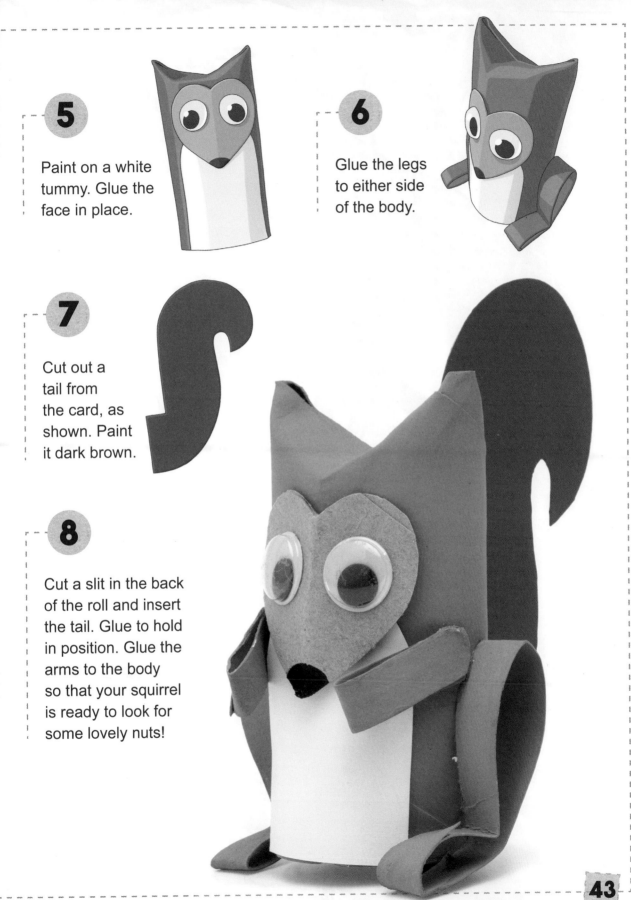

**5**

Paint on a white tummy. Glue the face in place.

**6**

Glue the legs to either side of the body.

**7**

Cut out a tail from the card, as shown. Paint it dark brown.

**8**

Cut a slit in the back of the roll and insert the tail. Glue to hold in position. Glue the arms to the body so that your squirrel is ready to look for some lovely nuts!

# Robin Finger Puppet

## You will need

**Two toilet rolls**

**Brown and black paint**

**Four googly eyes**

**Red, brown, yellow, white and green felt**

**1**

Flatten one end of a toilet roll and glue the sides together.

**2**

Paint the toilet roll brown. Cut out a red circle from felt and glue it to the front of the roll.

**3**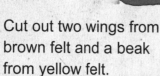

Cut out two wings from brown felt and a beak from yellow felt.

**4**

Glue the wings and beak in place. Cut out some green circles of felt and add them and the eyes, as shown. Now make a cute penguin by using different colours!

# spotty snake

## You will need

Six toilet rolls    Red and
                    blue felt
    Paint
                    Two googly
    Ribbon           eyes

**1** Paint six toilet rolls different bright colours.

**2** Cut off the corner of one roll, for the tail, as shown. Glue a piece of ribbon to the inside.

**3** Thread on the remaining rolls. Glue the ribbon to the inside of the last roll.

**4**

Flatten the last roll and glue the sides together to make a head. Add a strip of red felt for the tongue, some blue felt circles and a pair of googly eyes. Decorate your snake – it's ready to slither away!

# Butterfly

**This pretty butterfly will look great hanging from a window.**

**1**

Cut a toilet roll into six sections.

**2**

Paint four of them one colour and the other two a contrasting colour.

**3**

Squeeze the circles to make the tips pointed. Glue two circles together, to make a pair of wings. Use clothes pegs to hold the wings in place while they dry.

**4**

Glue the wings to the body.

**5**

Cut the remaining purple circle in half. Glue together to make antennae.

**6**

Glue the antennae in place. Add some string and hang your pretty butterfly in your room.

# Crab

## You will need

**Two toilet rolls**
**Orange paint**
**Thick card**
**Two googly eyes**

**1**

Paint a toilet roll orange. When dry, push the sides into the centre, to create a curved top. Repeat at the other end.

**2**

For the legs, cut another toilet roll into six circles and paint orange.

**3**

Fold all the legs, as shown. Cut out two claws from the thick card and paint them orange.

**4**

Glue the legs to the base of the crab's shell.

**5**

Paint some spots on the shell. Glue on the claws and a pair of googly eyes.

## Handy Hint
Always wash your brushes after use.

# Stripey Zebra

Did you know that zebras have black and white stripes to help them to hide in a herd and keep them safe from predators?

## You will need

Five toilet rolls
Black and white paint
Googly eyes
Black card
Blue felt

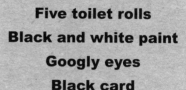

**1**

Cut the corner off one end of two toilet rolls.

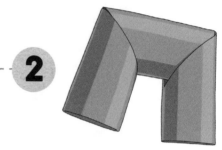

**2**

Glue the rolls to either end of another roll, as shown. They should slide into each other a bit.

**3**

Cut a ring from another roll and glue it to the body for the neck.

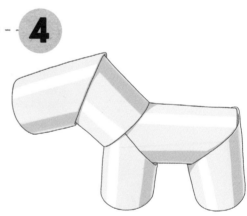

**4**

Cut the corner off another roll and glue it to the neck. This is the head. Paint your zebra white. When dry, paint on some stripes.

**Handy Hint**
The white paint must be completely dry before you add the stripes.

**5**

Cut a strip of black card and glue it along the back of the neck for the mane. Cut a strip of black card for the tail and glue it in place.

**6**

Cut out two ears from the card as well as a circle to make the nose. Cut out some blue felt circles and add them to the googly eyes. Glue everything in place and paint on a smile.

STRIPEY

# Kittens

## You will need

**Three toilet rolls**
**Paint**
**Thick card**
**White and pink felt**
**Six googly eyes**

**1**

For each cat, push the sides of a toilet roll into the centre, to create a curved top. Paint the roll.

**2**

Cut out a tail from thick card and paint it to match the body. You could add some stripes to the tail and body. Glue the tail to the back of the toilet roll.

**3**

Cut out a dome shape from a piece of white felt, and glue it to the front of the body.

**4**

Glue on a small triangle of pink felt, for the nose, and a pair of eyes. Draw on some whiskers with a black pen.

**5**

Repeat steps 1 to 4 to make two more cute little kittens.

# Pompom

**You will need**

Four toilet rolls
Paint
Glitter
Ribbon

**1**

Paint four rolls
inside and out,
using a contrasting
colour on the insides.

**2**

Fold the rolls
in half and glue the
middle together. Use a clothes
peg to hold in place until dry.

**3**

Glue the
four rolls together, into
a circle. Use clothes pegs
to hold in place until dry.

**4**

Add glittery spots to
decorate the pompom.
Add some ribbon
so you can hang up
your pompom in your
window to make a
pretty decoration.

# Cool Castle

## You will need

**Four long cardboard rolls**
**Eight toilet rolls**
**Blue and purple paint**
**Thick green card**
**Purple and grey card**

**1**

Paint the toilet rolls. Cut and assemble them to make a castle, as shown.

**2**

Cut two slits in one end of two short rolls. These will be the turrets.

**3**

Slide the turrets over the towers. Glue all the rolls to a piece of thick green card.

**4**

To make some roofs, cut a semi-circle of card for each tower, shape it into a cone and glue it in place. Paint the roofs.

**5**

Glue the roofs in place.

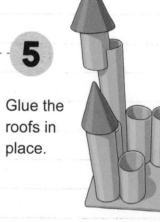

52

**6**

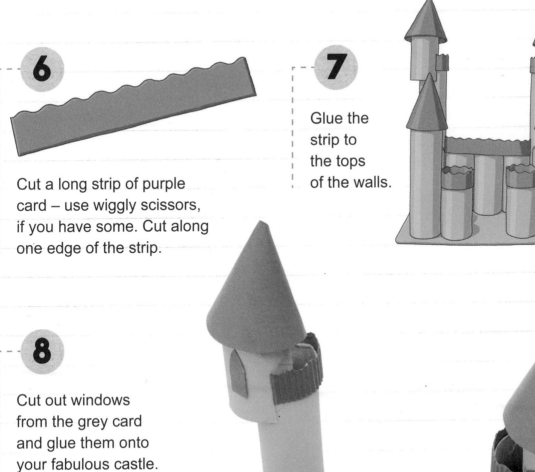

Cut a long strip of purple card – use wiggly scissors, if you have some. Cut along one edge of the strip.

**7**

Glue the strip to the tops of the walls.

**8**

Cut out windows from the grey card and glue them onto your fabulous castle.

**Handy Hint**

If you don't have the right colour card, you could use white card and paint it a colour you choose.

# Snappy Croc

Snap, snap, snap! This bright green crocodile friend is cute as can be but don't stand too close, or you'll become its tea!

**1**

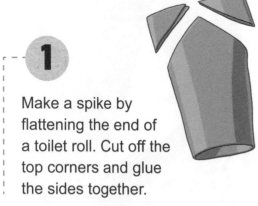

Make a spike by flattening the end of a toilet roll. Cut off the top corners and glue the sides together.

**2**

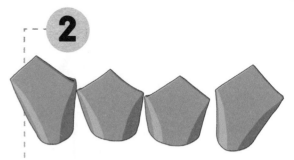

Make another spike of the same height. Make two more spikes, but slightly shorter. Paint them all green.

**3**

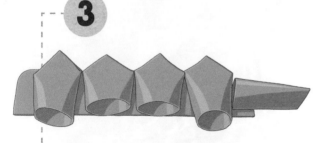

Flatten the top of another roll, glue the sides together and paint it green. This will be the tail. Cut two wedge-shaped lengths of thick card, and paint green. Glue the spikes and the tail onto the card, as shown. Make sure the two longer spikes extend below the bottom of the card. These will be legs. Glue the other piece of card to the opposite side.

**4**

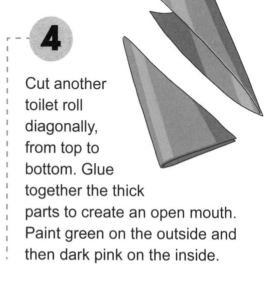

Cut another toilet roll diagonally, from top to bottom. Glue together the thick parts to create an open mouth. Paint green on the outside and then dark pink on the inside.

**5**

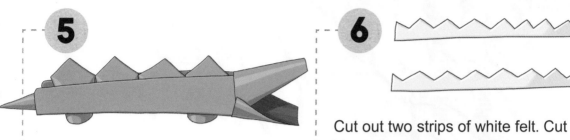

Glue the head onto the body.

**6**

Cut out two strips of white felt. Cut Vs along one edge to make teeth.

**7**

Glue the strips of felt along the inside of the mouth.

**8**

Paint on spots and add pink felt circles to the pair of googly eyes. Snap, snap, your croc is ready!

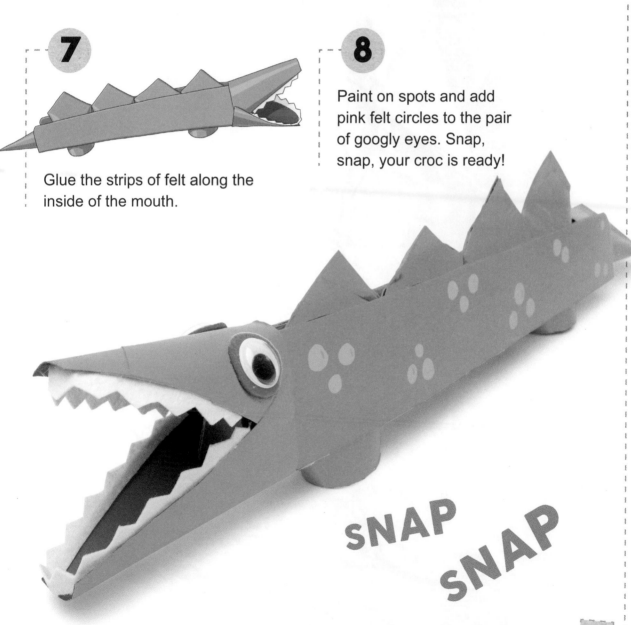

SNAP SNAP

# Pirate Skittles

## You will need

**Five toilet rolls**

**Paint, including pink and black**

**Felt**

**Paper**

**1**

Divide your toilet rolls into three sections. Paint the tops pink, the middles a bright colour and the bottoms black. Add spots or stripes to the middles.

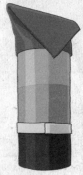

**2**

Cut out five large triangles of felt.

**3**

Wrap the long side of one triangle of felt around the pink end of one roll, and glue into position.

**4**

Fold down the tip of the triangle and glue. Repeat steps 3 and 4 on the other rolls.

**5**

Draw some features on each skittle. Scrunch up some paper, to make balls, then see how many skittles you can bowl over!

# Racing Cars

**1**

To make the body of each car, use a pencil to make a hole for your scissors to cut a flap, as shown. Fold the flap backwards. Paint the body.

**2**

Cut out four wheels from thick card and paint black with a white middle.

**3**

Use a pencil to make a hole in the middle of each wheel. Place the wheels against the car and make holes with the pencil again.

**4**

Use split pins to attach the wheels to the car.

**5**

Add a number and sporty stripes. Repeat the steps to make two more cars.

57

# Dinosaur Desk Tidy

## You will need

Three long cardboard rolls

Thick card

Pink felt

Five toilet rolls

Paint

Two googly eyes

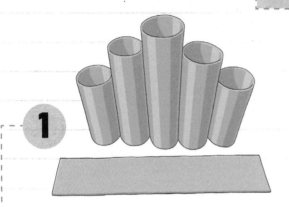

**1** Cut some of the rolls so that you have one long one, two shorter ones and two even shorter ones. Paint them and line them up, as shown. Glue them to thick card that is slightly longer than the row of rolls.

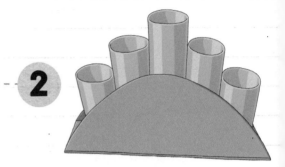

**2** Cut out two semi-circles of thick card. Paint them a contrasting colour. Glue them to either side of the row of rolls.

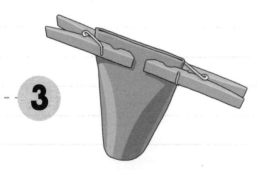

**3** Flatten the top of another roll, glue the sides together and paint it the same colour as the thick card in step 2. This will be the tail.

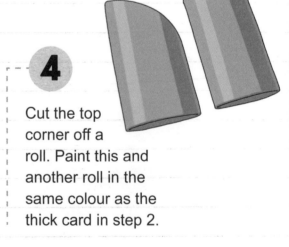

**4** Cut the top corner off a roll. Paint this and another roll in the same colour as the thick card in step 2.

**5**

Glue the rolls from step 4 together, for the head.

**6**

Glue the head and tail in place.

**7**

Paint on some spots and a smile. Add some felt circles and the eyes. Your happy dinosaur is ready to help you to tidy your desk!

DINO TIDY

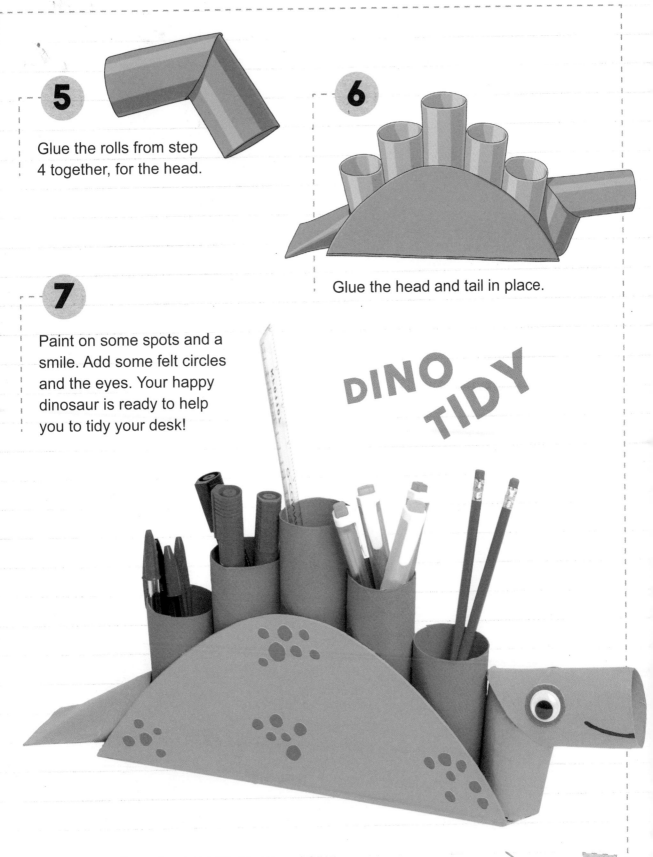

# Bunny Ears

## You will need

**Two long cardboard rolls**

**Grey and pink paint**

**Elastic**

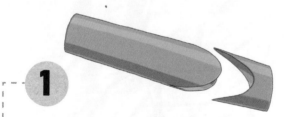

**1** Cut off the tops of the two cardboard rolls to leave a curved edge.

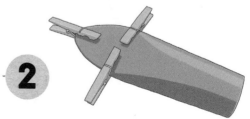

**2** Glue the top sides together. Hold in place with clothes pegs until dry.

**3** Paint the ears grey with a pink middle.

**4** Use a pencil to make a hole in either side of each ear.

**5** Thread a piece of elastic through the holes and tie a knot in the end. Hoppety-hop, your ears are ready to wear!

# Rocket

**1**

Paint a toilet roll in a lovely bright colour.

**2**

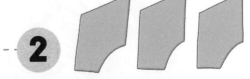

Cut out three pieces of thick card to make the legs and paint them.

**3**

Cut out a semi-circle from card and shape it into a cone.

5...4...3...
2...1...

**4**

Make three slits in the bottom of the roll. Glue the legs in place.

**5**

Glue on the cone. Add a window made from shiny card and some details. Get ready for lift-off!

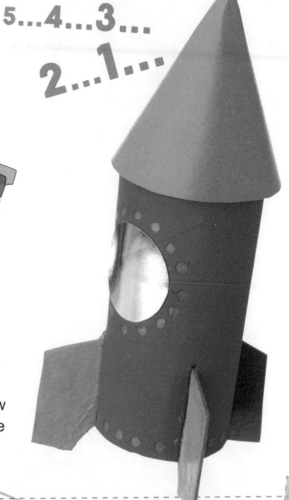

# Flamingo

Make this gorgeous pink flamingo and stand it proudly in your bathroom – but well away from the bath!

## You will need

**Three toilet rolls**

**Pink, black, yellow and white paint**

**Thick card**

**Six yellow straws**

**Blue felt**

**Two googly eyes**

**1**

Cut two rolls to make them slightly shorter. Cut the top corner off one of the rolls, to make it angled.

**2**

Paint the straight roll pink and the angled roll white with a black end. Glue the rolls together.

**3**

Paint another roll pink. Cut a slot in both pieces, as shown.

**4**

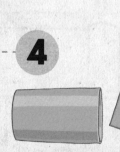

Paint a long strip of thick card pink. Glue the card into the two slots, at an angle, as shown.

**5**

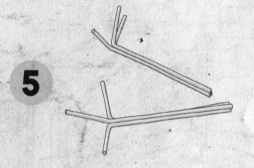

To make each leg, glue together the long parts of three bendy straws. Bend the short ends.

**6**

Use a pencil to make two holes in the bottom of the body.

**7**

Cut out two webbed feet from thick card, and paint yellow. Cut out a tail from thick card and paint pink.

**8**

Glue the webbed feet under the short pieces of straw. Insert the straws into the holes you made in the body. Glue to hold in position.

**9**

Cut a slot into the end of the body and slot the tail in place. Glue on some blue felt and googly eyes to complete the flamingo.

**Handy Hint**

To make eyes really stand out, use contrasting colours for your felt.

# Pretty Parrot

**Tropical birds are some of the prettiest creatures on Earth. Why not make this fun parrot and perch?**

## You will need

One long cardboard roll

Two toilet rolls

Paint, including brown

Thick card

Card

Blue felt

Googly eyes

**1**

Slightly flatten a long roll. Paint it red. Cut the top into a curved shape, as shown. Shape the bottom, as shown.

**2**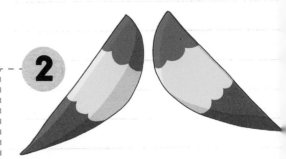

Cut out a pair of wings from thick card and paint them with bands of colour.

**3**

Cut out a beak from thick card and paint it. Glue the beak to the inside of the roll top. Glue the two sides of the roll top together, so the beak is sandwiched in the middle.

**4**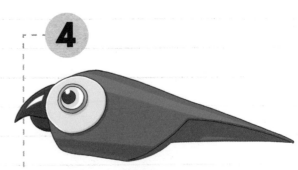

Cut out two circles of white card and glue to either side of the head. Glue on blue felt circles and googly eyes.

**5**

Glue the wings to the body, folding them out slightly.

**6**

Cut a narrow strip of card and glue it to the underside of the body.

**7**

To make the perch, cut a dip in one end of another toilet roll and glue another roll onto it. Paint brown.

SQUAWK!

**8**

Glue the parrot onto its perch – who's a pretty fellow then?

# Tree Shelf

Bring the outside indoors with this fun tree shelf. You can also keep pencils and pens inside it.

**You will need**

Twelve toilet rolls
Paint

**1**

Paint the outside of ten toilet rolls green. Paint the insides contrasting colours.

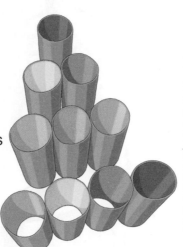

**2**

Glue the rolls together, to make a triangle.

**3**

Paint two more rolls brown and glue the sides together. Glue them to the base of your triangle.

**4**

You can make this tree as large as you like. Why not create an advent calendar and put little gifts in each roll?

# Reindeer Finger Puppet

## You will need

**One toilet roll**

**Light and dark brown paint**

**Thick card**

**Red felt**

**Two googly eyes**

**1** Paint a toilet roll brown.

**2** Cut out a pair of antlers and ears from thick card and paint.

**3** Glue the antlers to the inside of the roll. Flatten the top of the roll and glue to hold the sides together. Keep in place with clothes pegs.

**4** Cut out a dome from thick card.

**5** Glue the dome to the front and the ears to the top of the head. Add some googly eyes and a red felt nose. Rudolf is ready!

# Peacock

Proud as a peacock? You will
be when you have made this
dazzling creature.

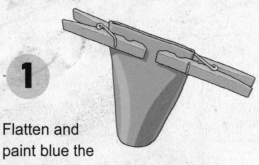

**1**

Flatten and
paint blue the
tops of eight toilet rolls. Glue one
end of each roll together. Use
pegs to hold in place until dry.

**2**

Glue the rolls together
to form a tail, as shown.

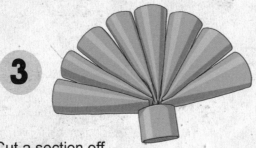

**3**

Cut a section off
another roll and glue it to the
bottom of the tail. Paint it blue.

**4**

Cut a body
from the thick
card and paint
it green-blue.

**5**

Glue the body
to the tail.

68

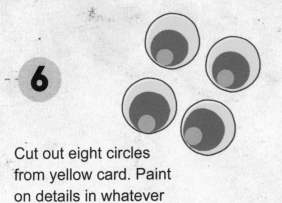

**6**

Cut out eight circles from yellow card. Paint on details in whatever colours you like.

**7**

Glue the circles onto the tail.

**8**

Cut a triangle from yellow card for the beak. Glue on a pair of googly eyes and your peacock is ready to parade!

# Plane

Zoom, zoom! Up, up and away!
Take to the skies with this
spectacular flying machine.

**1**

For the
body, paint
a toilet roll
orange.

**2**

From thick card cut a circle
to fit the top of the toilet roll.
Paint the circle orange. Then
cut a propeller from blue card.
Use a split pin to attach the
propeller to the circle, as shown.

**3**

Glue the
circle to one
end of the roll.

**4**

Cut out two
rectangles from thick card,
for the wings. Cut out three
smaller rectangles, each with
one curved corner, from thick
card. Paint all the pieces blue.

**5**

Glue the
body to one
of the wings.

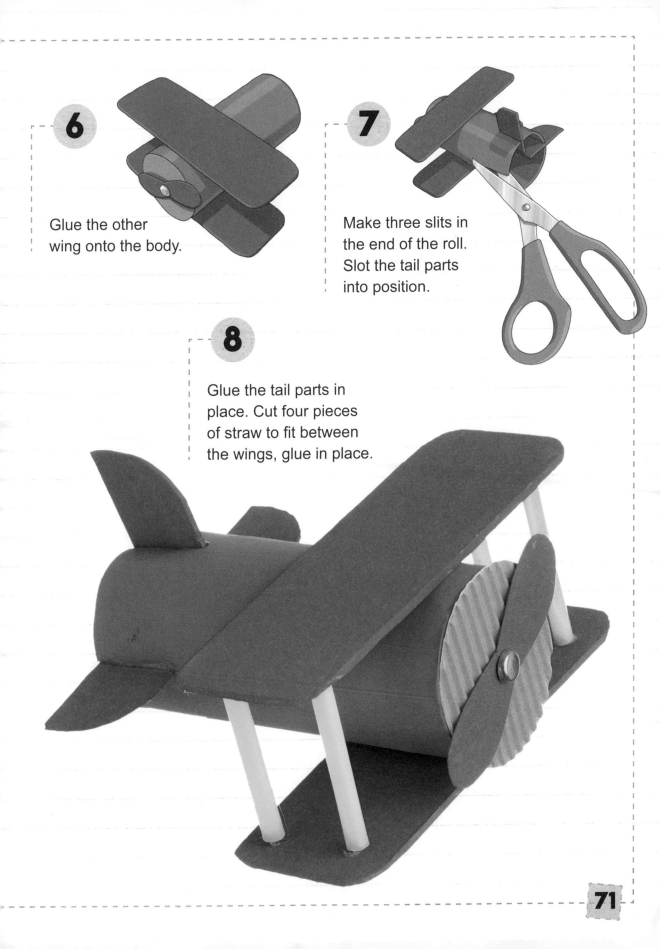

**6** Glue the other wing onto the body.

**7** Make three slits in the end of the roll. Slot the tail parts into position.

**8** Glue the tail parts in place. Cut four pieces of straw to fit between the wings, glue in place.

# Sheep

**You will need**

Three long
cardboard rolls

Five toilet rolls

White, grey and
black paint

Thick card

Card

Pink and green felt

Googly eyes

**1**

Cut a section off each long roll and
glue the rolls together. Glue two
sets of two shorter rolls together.

**2**

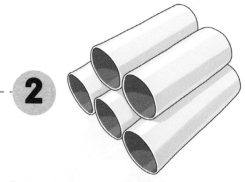

Paint the insides grey and the
outsides white. Glue one two-roll
piece to the three-roll piece as shown.

**3**

Glue the other two-roll
piece to the bottom of the
three-roll piece, as shown.

**4**

Cut out four legs
from thick card and paint black.

**5**

Glue the
legs in place.

**6**

Flatten the top of a roll and cut a curved top. Glue the top together.

**7**

Cut out a pair of ears from card and glue them to the head. Paint the head and ears black.

**8**

Glue the head to the front of the body. Add a pink felt nose, some green felt circles and some googly eyes. Your sheep is ready for the pasture!

BAAA

BAAA

# Cute Snail

There is nothing snail-paced about the speed at which you can make this cute little critter. Ready, steady, GO!

**1**

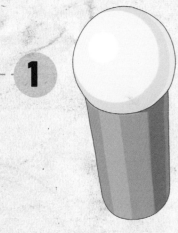

To make the head and body, glue a polystyrene ball to one end of a roll.

**2**

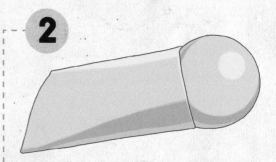

Flatten the other end of the toilet roll and glue the sides together. Paint the body and head a pale colour.

**3**

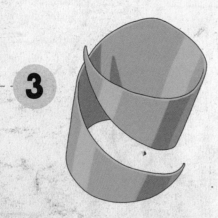

To make a shell, cut another roll into a spiral, following the line that runs around the roll.

**4**

Paint both sides. Roll one end and glue to the inside, as shown. Hold in place with a clothes peg.

**5**

Curl the roll into
a loose circle.
Glue the other end
to the outside of the
roll. Use a clothes peg
to hold in it place until dry.

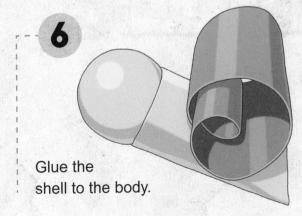

**6**

Glue the
shell to the body.

**7**

Use a pencil to make two holes
in the top of the head. Insert two
short pieces of straw and glue
into position. Add some felt
circles and googly eyes.
How fast can it go?

# Snowman

Brrr! Is it cold outside? Stay inside and make this cute snowman!

## You will need

Four toilet rolls

Black and white paint

Thick card

Two black pipe cleaners

Orange card

Felt

**1**

Leave two of the toilet rolls their full size, cut one slightly shorter than the first two and another one even shorter. Paint them all white.

**2**

Glue the two full rolls together. Glue the slightly shorter roll on top, as shown.

**3**

Glue the shortest roll to the very top. Use pegs to hold the rolls in place until dry.

**4**

Cut a circle from thick card just wider than a toilet roll. Paint that and the leftover shortest piece black.

**5**

Flatten the top of the black piece and glue the sides together. Glue the roll to the circle, as shown.

**6**

Glue the hat onto the body.

**7**

Make a pair of twig arms from pipe cleaners, and glue them to the snowman. Make a small cone from orange card for its nose, and glue it in place.

**8**

Cut a strip of felt and glue it around the neck, for a scarf. Draw on some eyes and a smile. Why not make a whole family of cute snowpeople?

**Handy Hint**

To make a cone, cut a quarter-circle and roll it round so that the straight edges meet.

# Santa

It's Christmas! Just don't put this Santa up your chimney!

## You will need

**One long cardboard roll**
**Red, pink and black paint**
**White card**
**One white pompom**
**One red pompom**
**Two googly eyes**

### 1

Fold over the top of a long cardboard roll. Glue to hold it in place.

### 2

Paint the top and middle parts red.

### 3

Paint a pink band between the red parts. Paint the bottom black.

### 4

Use wiggly scissors to cut a beard and two narrow strips of white card, for a fur trim.

**5**

Glue the beard and fur trims to the body.

HO HO HO

**6**

Add some googly eyes, a red pompom for the nose and a white pompom to the hat. Don't forget rosy cheeks and a smile before you put the finished Santa on your Christmas tree.

**Quarto Knows**

Quarto is the authority on a wide range of topics.

Quarto educates, entertains and enriches the lives of our readers—enthusiasts and lovers of hands-on living.

www.quartoknows.com

Publisher: Maxime Boucknooghe
Editorial Director: Victoria Garrard
Art Director: Miranda Snow
Editors: Sophie Hallam, Sarah Eason and Jennifer Sanderson
Designer: Paul Myerscough
Photographer: Michael Wicks
Illustrator: Tom Connell
With thanks to our wonderful models Islah, Ethan and Ania.

First published in the UK in 2016
by QED Publishing
Part of The Quarto Group
The Old Brewery, 6 Blundell Street
London, N7 9BH

A catalogue record for this book is available from the British Library.

ISBN 978 1 78493 558 0

Printed in China